T0387564

Momentous Materials
Steel

by Trudy Becker

www.focusreaders.com

Copyright © 2024 by Focus Readers®, Mendota Heights, MN 55120. All rights reserved. No part of this book may be reproduced or utilized in any form or by any means without written permission from the publisher.

Focus Readers is distributed by North Star Editions:
sales@northstareditions.com | 888-417-0195

Produced for Focus Readers by Red Line Editorial.

Photographs ©: Shutterstock Images, cover, 1, 4, 7, 8, 11, 13, 14, 17, 18, 20–21, 22, 25, 27, 29

Library of Congress Cataloging-in-Publication Data
Library of Congress Cataloging-in-Publication Data is available on the Library of Congress website.

ISBN
979-8-88998-037-7 (hardcover)
979-8-88998-080-3 (paperback)
979-8-88998-162-6 (ebook pdf)
979-8-88998-123-7 (hosted ebook)

Printed in the United States of America
Mankato, MN
012024

About the Author

Trudy Becker lives in Minneapolis, Minnesota. She likes exploring new places and loves anything involving books.

Table of Contents

CHAPTER 1
Across the Bridge 5

CHAPTER 2
History of Steel 9

CHAPTER 3
Modern Methods 15

THAT'S AMAZING!
Strong and Beautiful 20

CHAPTER 4
Steel World 23

Focus on Steel • 28
Glossary • 30
To Learn More • 31
Index • 32

Chapter 1

Across the Bridge

A crane lifts a large sheet of metal. Workers fit the metal into place. They are building a **suspension bridge**. It will cross a river. The bridge's long **cables** are made of steel. So are many other parts.

Steel bridges are very strong. They can support the weight of many heavy vehicles.

5

The steel started out as iron ore. Factory workers melted it. Next, they added and removed materials. Then they shaped it. The steel came a long way before reaching the building site.

After a few months, the bridge is finished. The city hosts a

In 2022, a new bridge opened in Turkey. It set a record for the longest suspension bridge. It was 6,637 feet (2,023 m) long.

 The 1915 Çanakkale Bridge in Turkey crosses from Europe to Asia.

grand opening. Trucks and cars drive across. It would not be possible without steel. People use this material to create many amazing structures.

Chapter 2

History of Steel

Humans have used steel for thousands of years. In ancient Turkey, people worked with steel tools. Ancient Romans used steel weapons. Some types of steel from ancient India are still used today.

In ancient Rome, soldiers fought with swords made of steel.

By the mid-1700s, people were discovering new methods. A clockmaker in England created one new kind of steel. It was called crucible steel. People found out that it was strong and useful. So, they copied his method. This type of steel became common.

In the 1800s, railroad production was growing. The train tracks were often built with iron or wood. Steel made better tracks. But it was difficult to produce. It was

 A crucible is a container that holds melted metal.

also expensive. People needed a better way.

A breakthrough came in 1855. An inventor named Henry Bessemer found a cheap method for making steel. It was fast, too. As a result, steel production grew rapidly.

Steel production increased even more in the 1900s. Two world wars took place. Armies around the world needed materials. Factories churned out steel weapons. They made steel war machines. During this time, steel technology improved.

A company called US Steel was created in 1901. It became the first company worth $1 billion.

 Factories produced thousands of steel tanks during World War II (1939–1945).

Soon, people could use steel for even more purposes. People created steel skyscrapers. They built advanced steel bridges. And homes were filled with machines that used steel.

Chapter 3

Modern Methods

Steel starts off as iron ore. Large furnaces heat it. That causes it to melt. Then, some impurities are removed. These are things that would make the steel weaker.

Furnaces for making steel can reach 2,750 degrees Fahrenheit (1,510°C).

Other ingredients can be added at this time. Tungsten is one example. This metal can make steel harder. When the whole mixture is ready, the steel is cooled. Workers form it into shape.

For many years, Bessemer's method was common. But new ways have mostly replaced it. One method uses electric currents to melt materials. Another method adds oxygen very quickly. That helps remove impurities. This

 All types of steel are alloys. An alloy is a metal mixed with other materials.

process is cheap and fast. As a result, it has become the most popular.

These new methods helped steel grow. Production tripled between 1970 and 2020.

17

 Today, approximately 60 percent of steel is recycled.

However, there is a major problem. Making steel uses lots of energy. And most of the energy comes from **fossil fuels**. When these fuels burn, they release gases that warm the planet. That is causing **climate change**.

Fortunately, steel is easy to recycle. It can be melted into **scrap**. Then, it can be reformed. The steel does not lose its good qualities. So, steel scrap is widely used and reused.

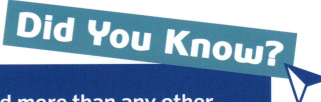

Steel is recycled more than any other material in the world.

THAT'S AMAZING!

Strong and Beautiful

Inventors created stainless steel in the early 1900s. To make it, an ingredient called chromium is added. It helps protect the steel from rust and stains.

Stainless steel became hugely popular. People liked it for many reasons. One reason is its strength. For example, it can safely contain **toxic** materials. That way, these materials cannot get out into the environment.

Stainless steel is also beautiful. Chromium gives it a shiny surface. That makes it popular in homes and offices.

Many kitchen items are made with stainless steel.

Chapter 4

Steel World

Some of steel's most common uses are in **transportation**. Many car parts are made from steel. Planes and ships are built with steel, too. So are most shipping containers. They are usually large steel boxes.

 Cars are made of steel. So are the machines that make them.

23

Appliances are another common use. Many homes have washing machines and dryers. Those machines often use steel parts. So do microwaves, refrigerators, and dishwashers. Steel is also part of the machines that create those things. So, steel machines help people make more steel machines.

Did You Know?

Steel can be used for art. Many artists use it to make sculptures.

 The Kelpies is a huge statue in Scotland.

In all these ways, steel is very useful. Demand for steel is likely to keep growing. But steel-making still harms the planet. So, scientists want to improve it.

25

Usually, making steel releases large amounts of carbon dioxide. But scientists are trying to make the process **carbon-neutral**. They hope it can take in as much carbon as it releases. Other scientists are working on different methods. They want to create new processes using hydrogen or electricity.

These new methods are not cheap. Research could cost trillions of dollars. Updating machines would be hard, too. It will take

 Steel enables people to build skyscrapers that are thousands of feet tall.

time for things to change. In the meantime, steel use will continue. Steel is still a building block of the modern world.

27

FOCUS ON
Steel

Write your answers on a separate piece of paper.

1. Write a few sentences describing the main ideas of Chapter 4.

2. Which use of steel do you think is the most important? Why?

3. When was crucible steel first created?
   A. in ancient times
   B. in the 1700s
   C. in the 2020s

4. Stainless steel does not get rusty or stained. Why is that useful?
   A. The steel is harder to make that way.
   B. The steel can last for a longer time.
   C. The steel can be used in fewer places.

5. What does **breakthrough** mean in this book?

*A **breakthrough** came in 1855. An inventor named Henry Bessemer found a cheap method for making steel. It was fast, too.*

    A. a vehicle that moves quickly
    B. a war that kills many people
    C. a major discovery

6. What does **impurities** mean in this book?

*Then, some **impurities** are removed. These are things that would make the steel weaker.*

    A. parts that are different and not needed
    B. parts that make things stronger
    C. the most important ingredients

Answer key on page 32.

Glossary

appliances
Machines used in the home, such as toasters and refrigerators.

cables
Thick, strong pieces of wire.

carbon-neutral
Having a balance between how much carbon is released and how much is taken in.

climate change
A human-caused global crisis involving long-term changes in Earth's temperature and weather patterns.

fossil fuels
Energy sources that come from the remains of plants and animals that died long ago.

scrap
Metal that is no longer needed and can be used again.

suspension bridge
A kind of bridge that hangs from cables that are attached to towers.

toxic
Harmful or poisonous.

transportation
A system for moving people and goods from one place to another.

To Learn More

BOOKS

Kenney, Karen Latchana. *Building a Roller Coaster.* Mankato, MN: Amicus, 2019.

Murray, Julie. *Charles Kuonen Suspension Bridge.* Minneapolis: Abdo Publishing, 2019.

Petrie, Sean. *Welders on the Job.* Mankato, MN: The Child's World, 2020.

NOTE TO EDUCATORS

Visit **www.focusreaders.com** to find lesson plans, activities, links, and other resources related to this title.

Index

A
appliances, 24

B
Bessemer, Henry, 11, 16

C
chromium, 20
climate change, 19
crucible steel, 10

F
fossil fuels, 18–19

H
hydrogen, 26

I
impurities, 15–16
iron, 6, 10, 15

M
machines, 12–13, 24, 26
melting, 6, 15–16, 19

O
oxygen, 16

R
recycling, 19
Romans, 9

S
skyscrapers, 13
stainless steel, 20
suspension bridge, 5–6

T
tungsten, 16

W
weapons, 9, 12

Answer Key: 1. Answers will vary; **2.** Answers will vary; **3.** B; **4.** B; **5.** C; **6.** A